T0045637

CHRISTMAS SONGBOOK FOR CHILDREN

ISBN 978-0-634-01684-4

Walt Disney Music Company
Wonderland Music Company, Inc.

DISTRIBUTED BY

HAL•LEONARD®
CORPORATION
7777 W. BLUEMOUND RD. P.O. BOX 13819 MILWAUKEE, WI 53213

Visit Hal Leonard Online at
www.halleonard.com

AS LONG AS THERE'S CHRISTMAS

CHRISTMAS

from Walt Disney's BEAUTY AND THE BEAST - THE ENCHANTED CHRISTMAS

Words by RACHEL PORTMAN
Lyrics by DON BLACK

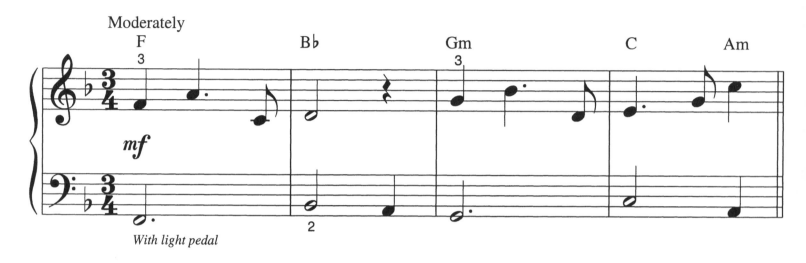

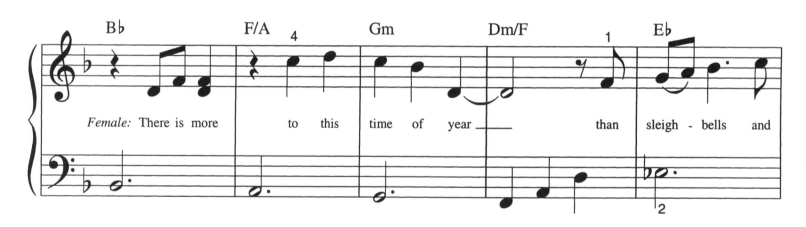

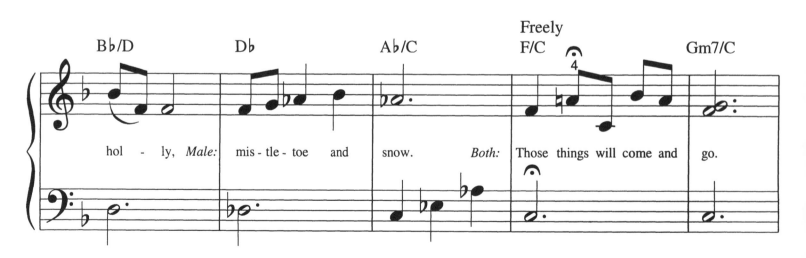

4

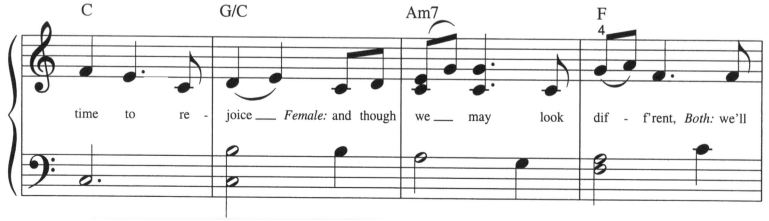

DEAR SANTA

Words and Music by MICHAEL SILVERSHER
and PATTY SILVERSHER

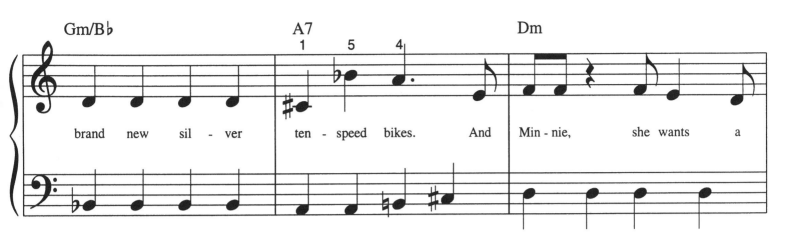

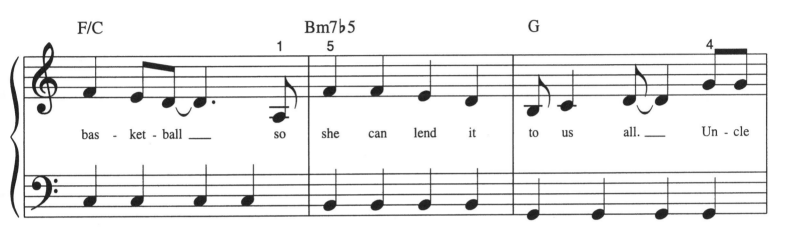

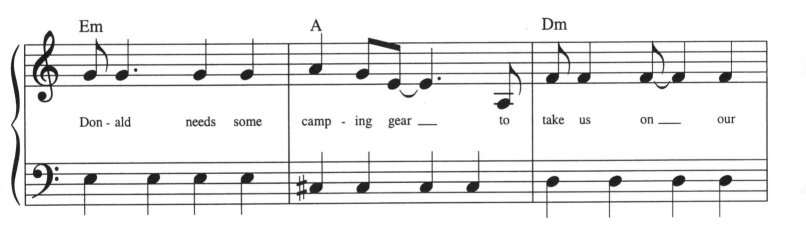

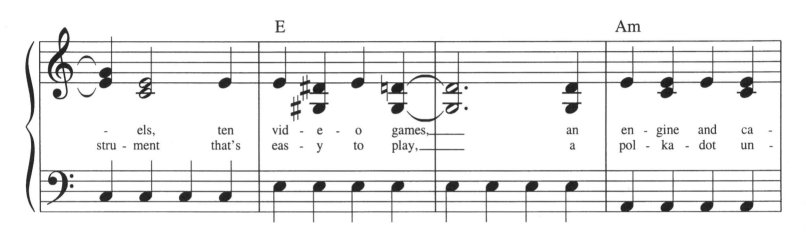

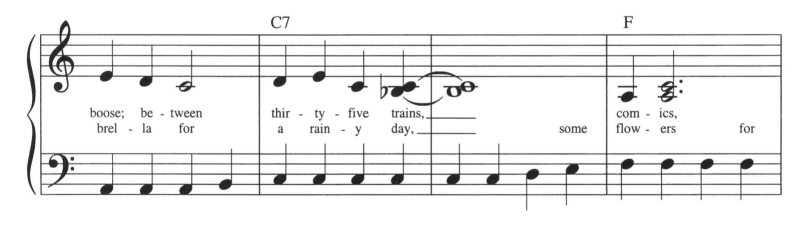

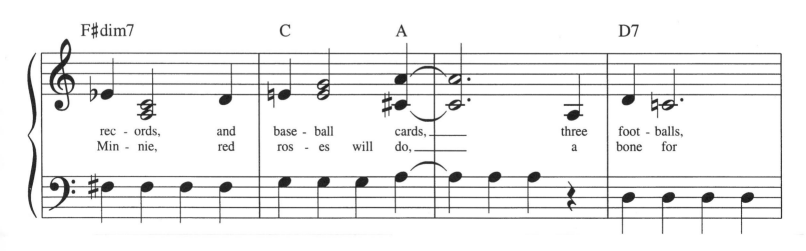

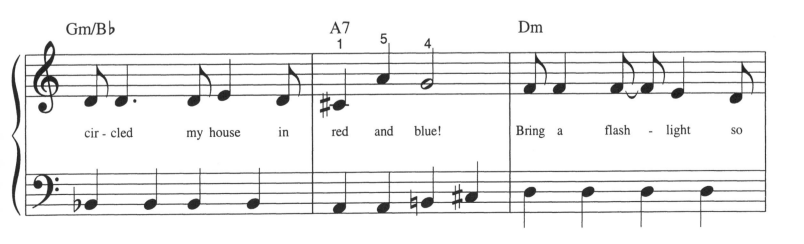

CODA

DECK THE HALL

Traditional Welsh Carol

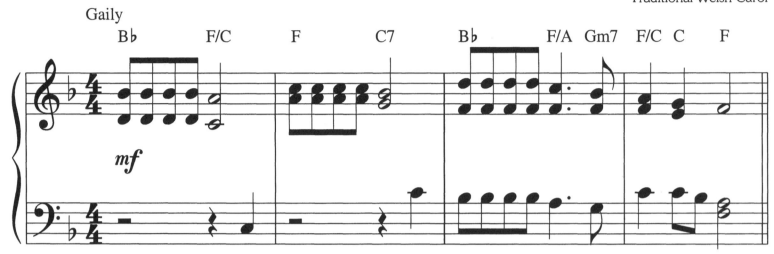

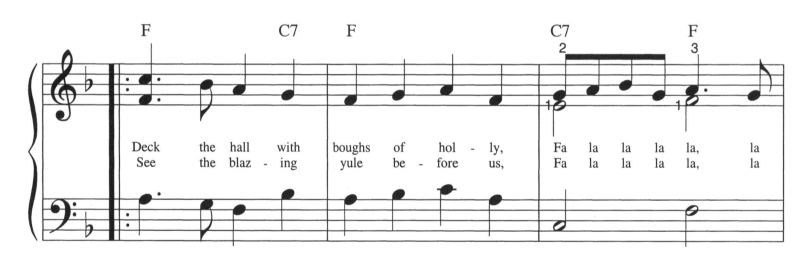

Deck the hall with boughs of hol - ly, Fa la la la la, la

See the blaz - ing yule be - fore us, Fa la la la la, la

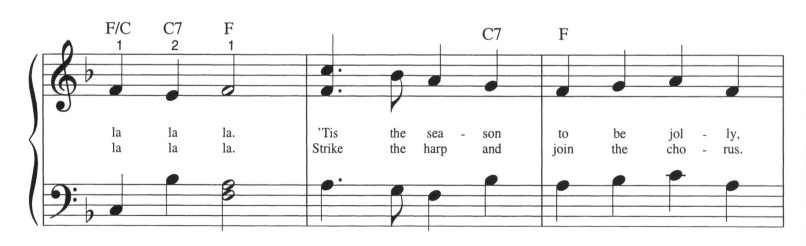

la la la. 'Tis the sea - son to be jol - ly,

la la la. Strike the harp and join the cho - rus.

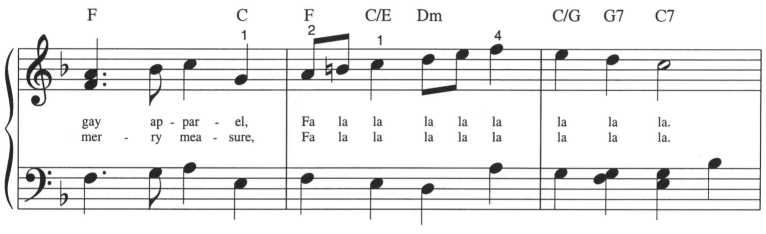

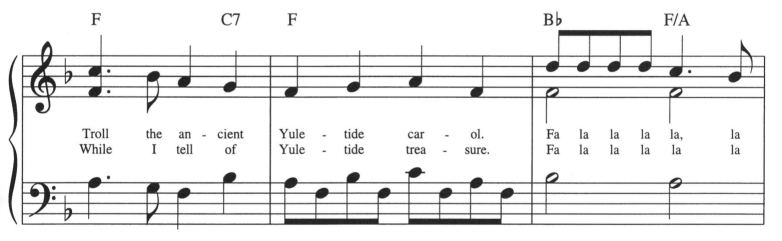

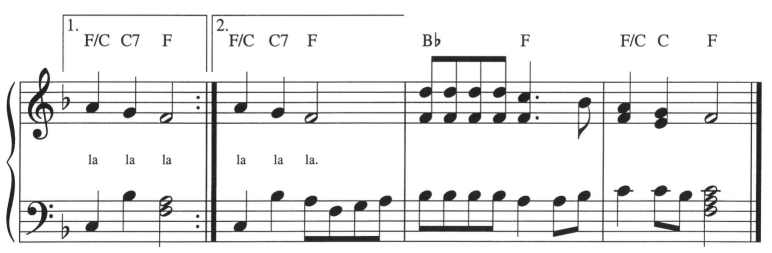

DING DONG! MERRILY ON HIGH!

French Carol

GOOD KING WENCESLAS

Words by JOHN M. NEALE
Music by PIAE CANTIONES

With spirit

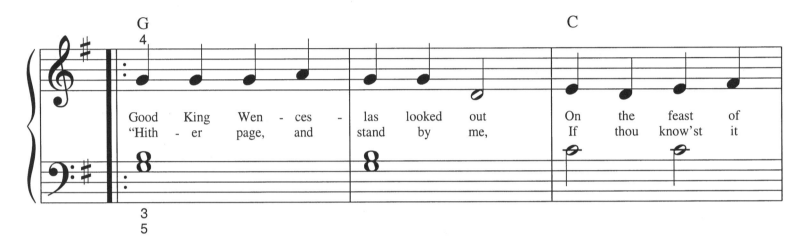

Good King Wen - ces - las looked out
"Hith - er page, and stand by me,
On the feast of
If thou know'st it

Steph - en,
tell - ing,
When the snow lay
Yon - der peas - ant,
round a - bout,
who is he?

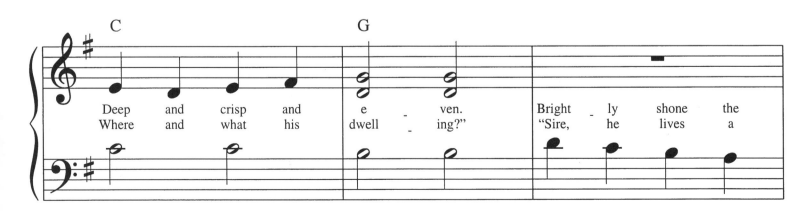

Deep and crisp and e - ven.
Where and what his dwell - ing?"
Bright - ly shone the
"Sire, he lives a

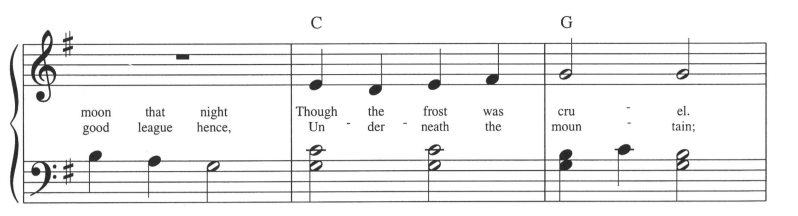

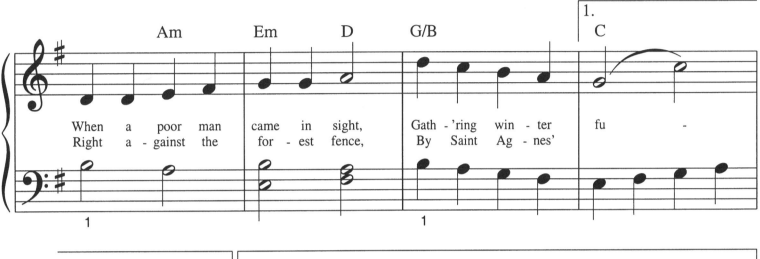

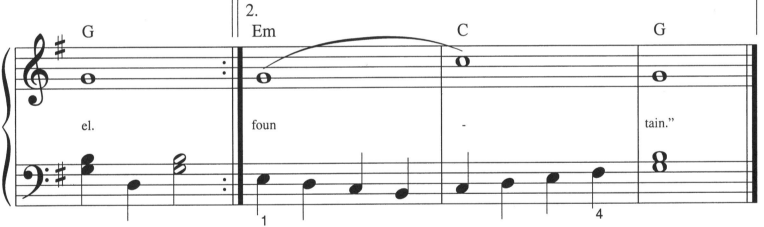

3. "Bring me flesh, and bring me wine,
   Bring me pine-logs hither;
   Thou and I will see him dine,
   When we bear them thither."
   Page and monarch forth they went,
   Forth they went together;
   Through the rude winds wild lament
   And the bitter weather.

4. "Sire, the night is darker now,
   And the wind blows stronger;
   Fails my heart, I know not how,
   I can go no longer."
   "Mark my footsteps, my good page,
   Tread thou in them boldly;
   Thou shall find the winter's rage
   Frees they blood less coldly."

5. In his master's steps he trod,
   Where the snow lay dinted;
   Heat was in the very sod
   Which the saint had printed
   Therefore, Christian men, be sure,
   Wealth or rank possessing,
   Ye who now will bless the poor,
   Shall yourselves find blessing.

I HEARD THE BELLS
ON CHRISTMAS DAY

Words by HENRY WADSWORTH LONGFELLOW
Music by JOHN BAPTISTE CALKIN

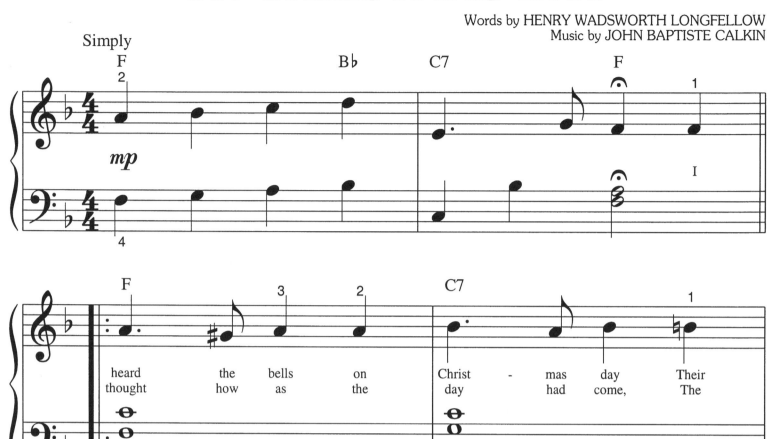

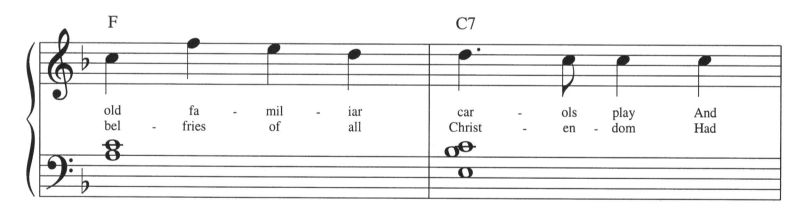

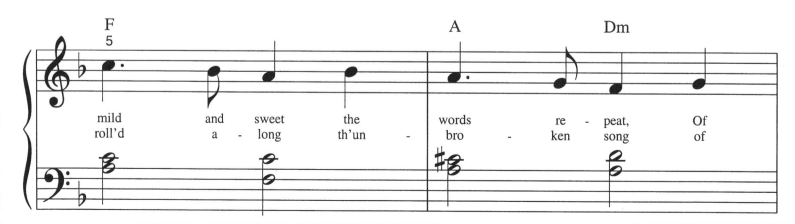

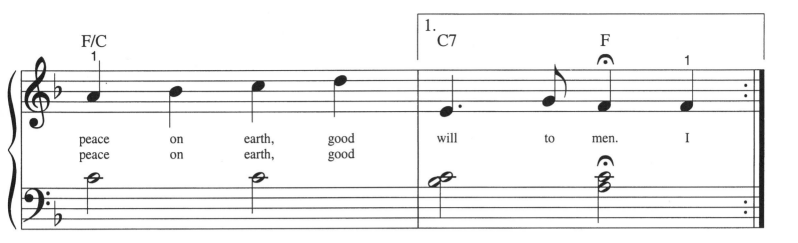

peace   on   earth,   good   will   to   men.   I
peace   on   earth,   good

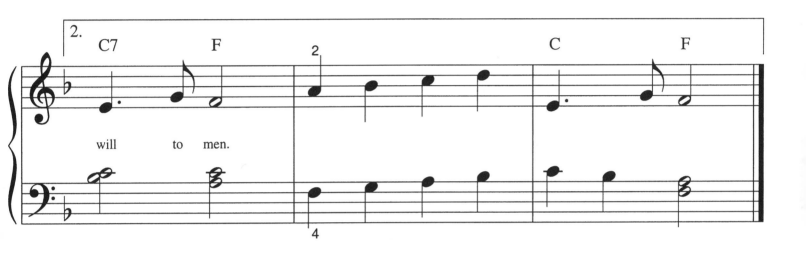

will   to   men.

3. And in despair I bowed my head:
    "There is no peace on earth," I said,
    "For hate is strong and mocks the song
    Of peace on earth, good will to men."

4. Then pealed the bells more loud an deep
    "God is not dead, nor does He sleep;
    The wrong shall fail, the right prevail,
    With peace on earth, good will to men."

5. Till, ringing on its way
    The world revolved from night to day,
    A voice, a chime, a chant sublime,
    Of peace on earth, good will to men!

JINGLE BELLS/
SLEIGH RIDE THROUGH THE SNOW

Words and Music by ANDY DiTARANTO
and SAMUEL J. WISNER

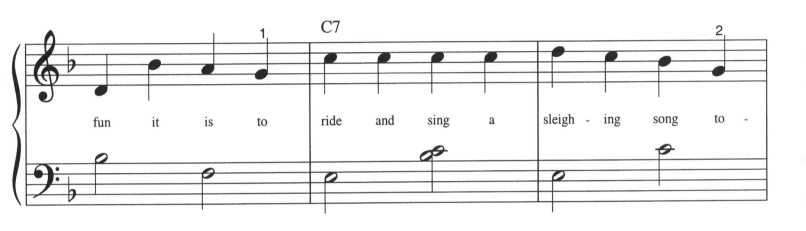

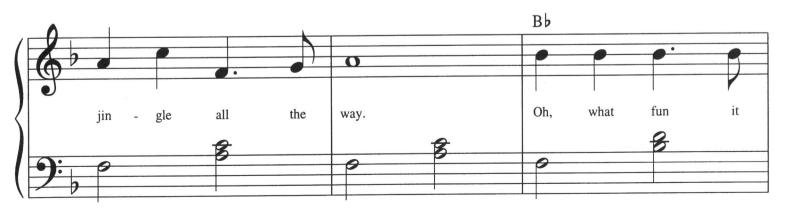

is to ride in a one - horse o - pen sleigh. _____

Jin - gle bells, jin - gle bells, jin - gle all the way.

Oh, what fun it is to ride in a one - horse o - pen

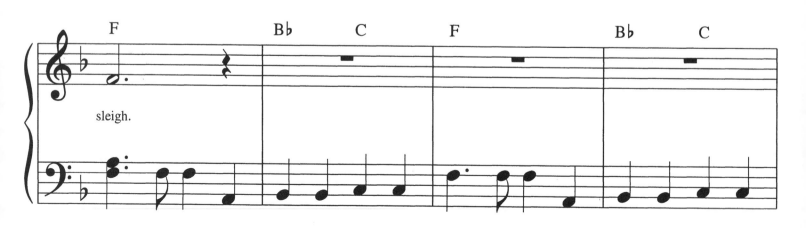

sleigh.

SLEIGH RIDE THROUGH THE SNOW

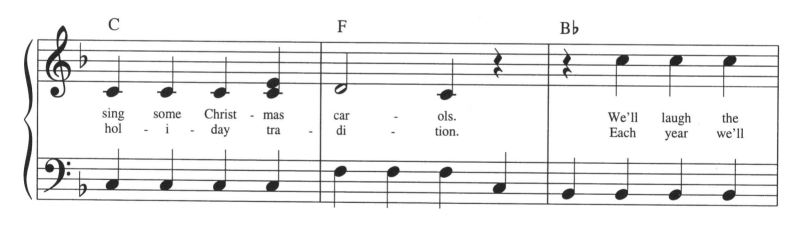

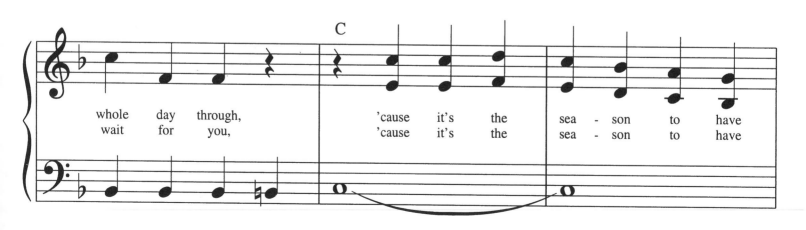

JOLLY OLD ST. NICHOLAS

Traditional 19th Century American Carol

Moderately Slow

mf

Jol - ly old Saint Ni - cho - las,

lean your ear this way, Don't you tell a

sin - gle soul what I'm going to say.

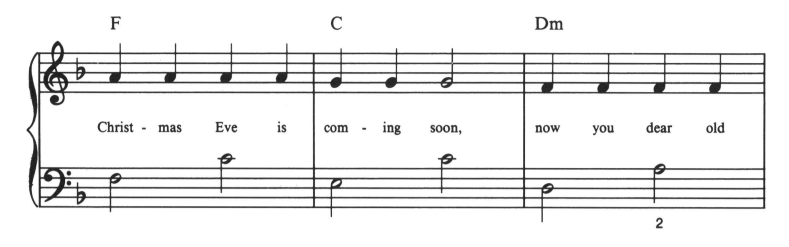

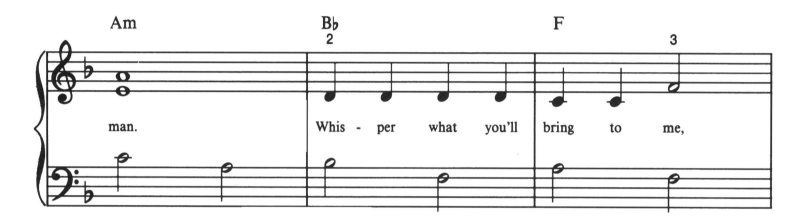

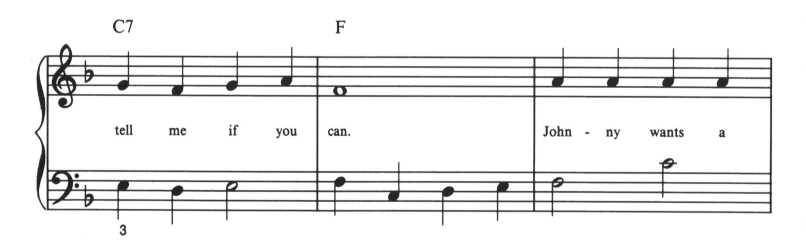

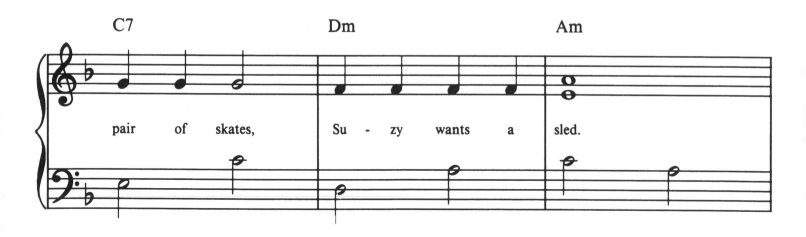

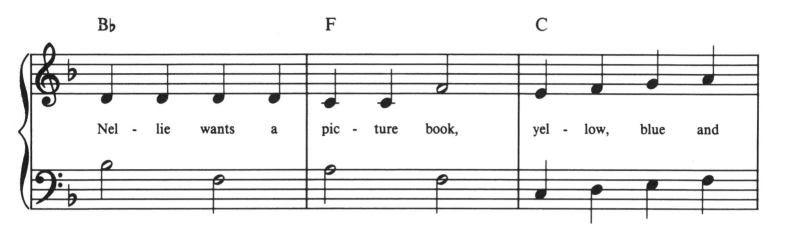

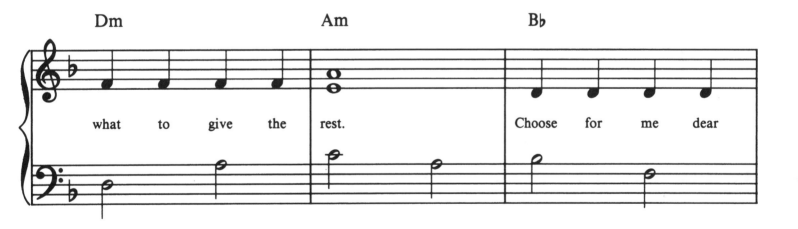

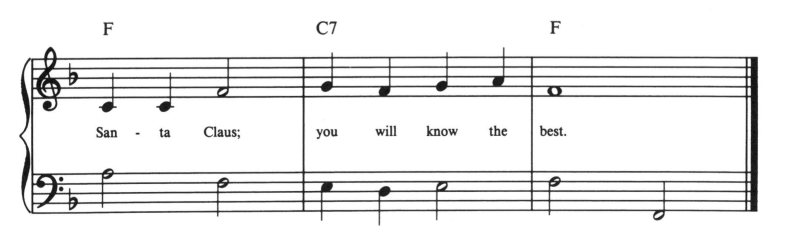

O CHRISTMAS TREE

Traditional German Carol

'TWAS THE NIGHT BEFORE CHRISTMAS

Words by CLEMENT CLARK MOORE
Music by F. HENRI KLICKMAN

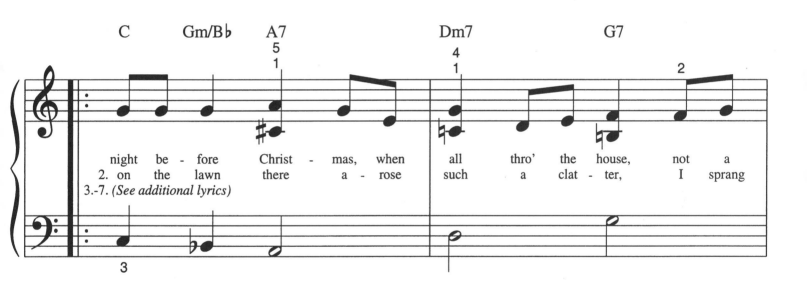

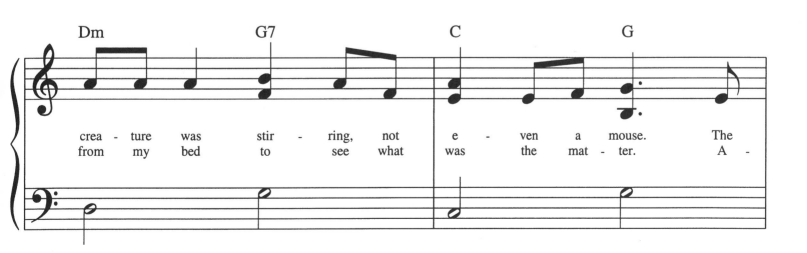

1. 'Twas the
night be - fore Christ - mas, when all thro' the house, not a
2. on the lawn there a - rose such a clat - ter, I sprang
3.-7. (See additional lyrics)

crea - ture was stir - ring, not e - ven a mouse. The
from my bed to see what was the mat - ter. A -

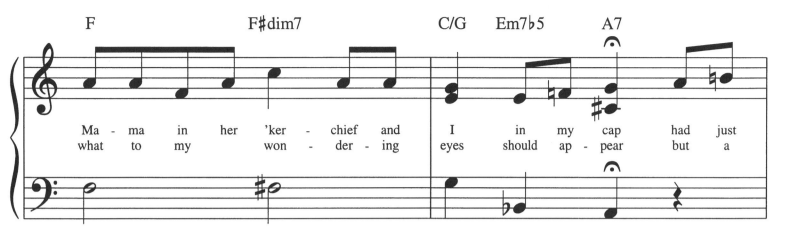

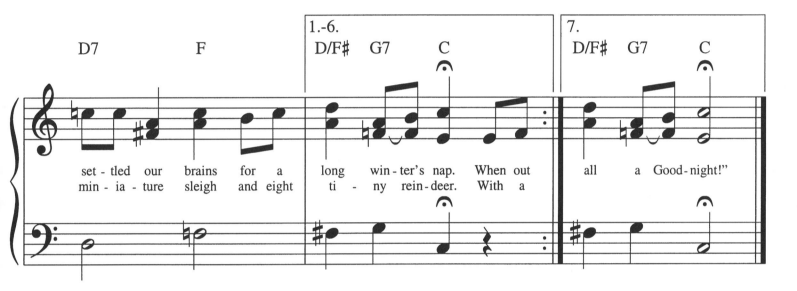

Additional Lyrics

3. With a little old driver, so lively and quick,
   I knew in a moment it must be St. Nick.
   More rapid than eagles his coursers they came,
   And he whistled, and shouted, and called them by name:
   "Now, Dasher! now, Dancer now, Prancer! now Vixen
   On, Comet! on, Cupid! on Donder and Blitzen!
   To the top of the porch, to the top of the wall!
   Now dash away, dash away, dash away all!"

4. As dry leaves that before the wild hurricane fly,
   When they meet with an obstacle, mount to the sky,
   So up to the house-top the coursers they flew,
   With the sleigh full of toys, and St. Nicholas, too.
   And then in a twinkling I heard on the roof
   The prancing and pawing of each little hoof.
   As I drew in my head, and was turning around,
   Down the chimney St. Nicholas came with a bound.

5. He was dressed all in fur from head to his foot,
   And his clothes were all tarnished with ashes and soot;
   A bundle of toys he had flung on his back,
   And he look like a peddler just opening his pack
   His eyes how they twinkled! his dimples how merry!
   His cheeks were like roses, his noses like a cherry,
   His droll little mouth was drawn up like a bow,
   And the beard of his chin was as white as the snow.

6. The stump of a pipe he held tight in his teeth,
   And the smoke, it encircled his head like a wreath.
   He had a broad face, and a round little belly
   That shook, when he laughed, like a bowl full of jelly.
   He was chubby and plump - a right jolly old elf -
   And I laughed when I saw him, in spite of myself.
   A wink of his eye, and a twist of his head,
   Soon gave me to know I had nothing to dread.

7. He spoke not a word, but went straight to his work,
   And filled all the stockings; then turned with a jerk,
   And laying his finger aside of his nose,
   And giving a nod, up the chimney he rose.
   He sprang to his sleigh, to his team gave a whistle,
   And away they all fled like the down of a thistle;
   But I heard him exclaim, ere he drove out of sight -
   "Happy Christmas to all, and to all a Good-night!"

OH, WHAT A MERRY
CHRISTMAS DAY

from Walt Disney's MICKEY'S CHRISTMAS CAROL

Words and Music by IRWIN KOSTAL
and FREDERICK SEARLES

PARADE OF THE WOODEN SOLDIERS

English Lyrics by BALLARD MacDONALD
Music by LEON JESSEL

sab - res a - clink - ing, sol - diers a - wink - ing at each pret - ty

Em

lit - tle maid. Here they come! Here they come! Here they come! Here they come,

1

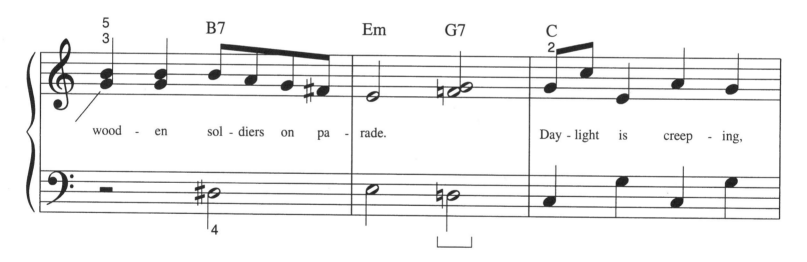

5
3

B7

Em

G7

C
2

wood - en sol - diers on pa - rade. Day - light is creep - ing,

4

G7

dol - lies are sleep - ing, in the toy - shop win - dow fast;

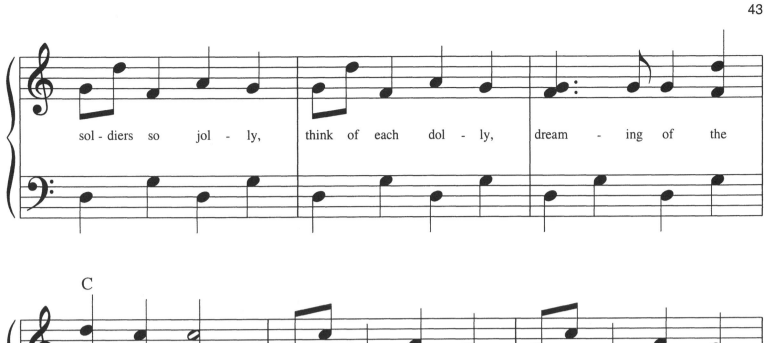

sol - diers so jol - ly, think of each dol - ly, dream - ing of the

night that's past. When in the morn - ing, with - out a warn - ing,

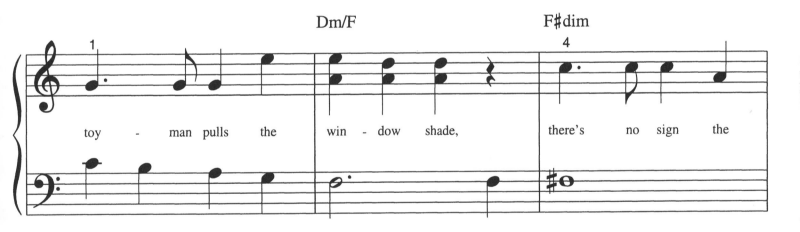

toy - man pulls the win - dow shade, there's no sign the

Wood bri - gade was ev - er out up - on pa - rade.

SNOW HO HO

Words and Music by
ROBIN FREDERICK

45

46

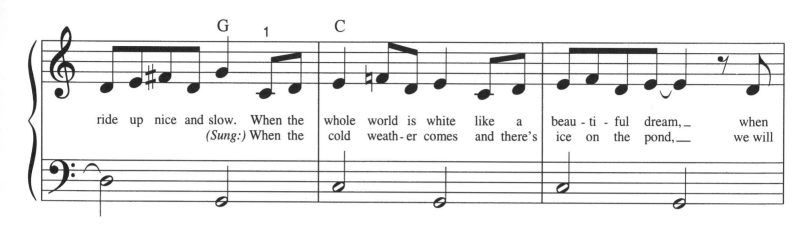

ride up nice and slow. When the whole world is white like a beau-ti-ful dream, __ when
(Sung:) When the cold weath-er comes and there's ice on the pond, __ we will

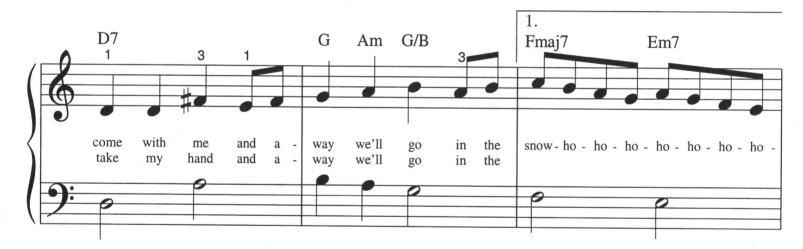

snow - flakes take flight and i - ci - cles gleam, __ then
glide, we will slide through the trees and be - yond. __ So,

come with me and a - way we'll go in the snow-ho-ho-ho-ho-ho-ho-ho-
take my hand and a - way we'll go in the

ho - ho - ho - ho - ho, in the snow.

TOYLAND
from BABES IN TOYLAND

Words by GLEN MacDONOUGH
Music by VICTOR HERBERT

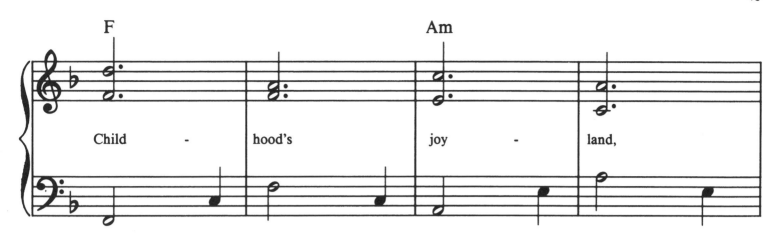

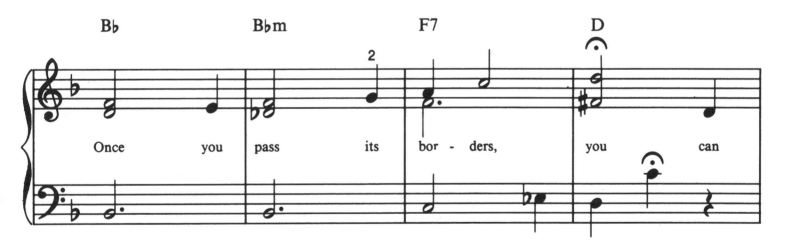

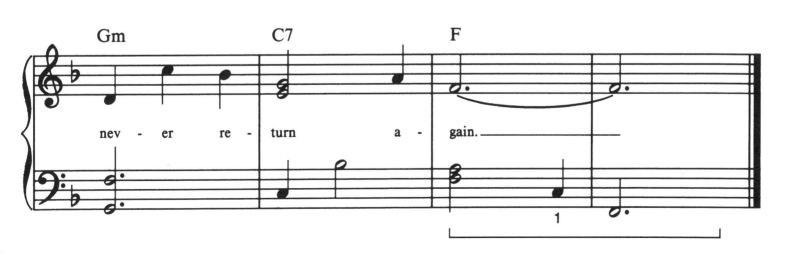

UP ON THE HOUSETOP

Words and Music by
B.R. HANDY

Brightly

Up on the house - top the rein - deer pause, Out jumps good old

San - ta Claus; Down thru the chim - ney with lots of toys,

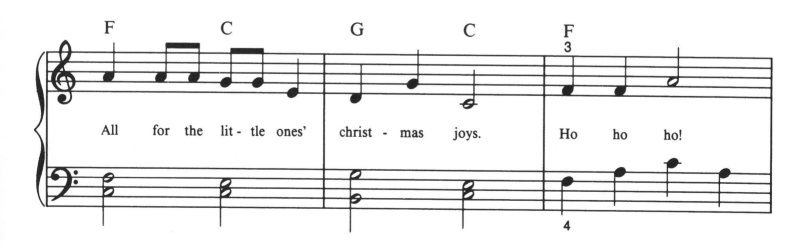

All for the lit - tle ones' christ - mas joys. Ho ho ho!

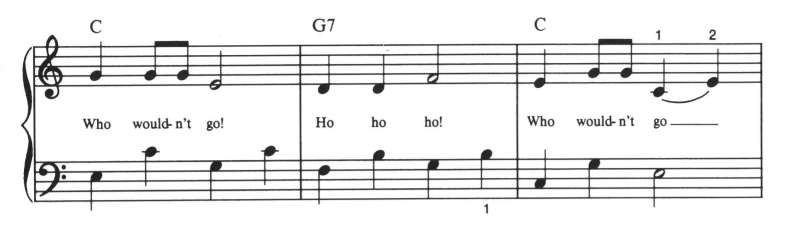

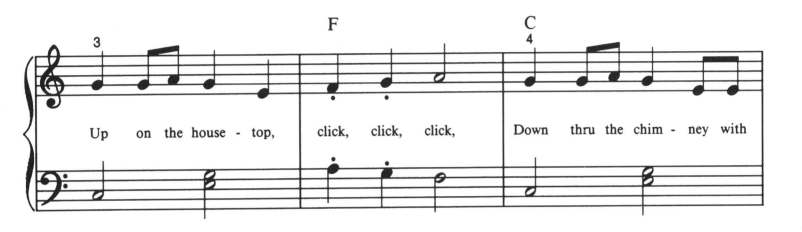

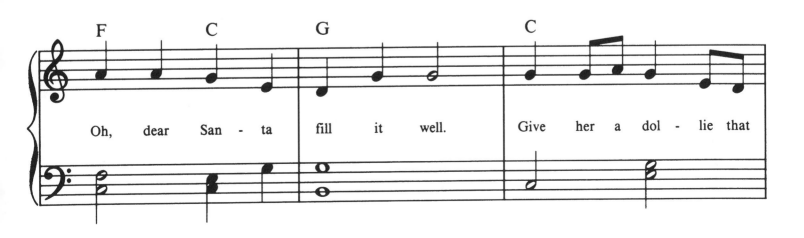

WE WISH YOU A MERRY CHRISTMAS

Traditional English Folksong

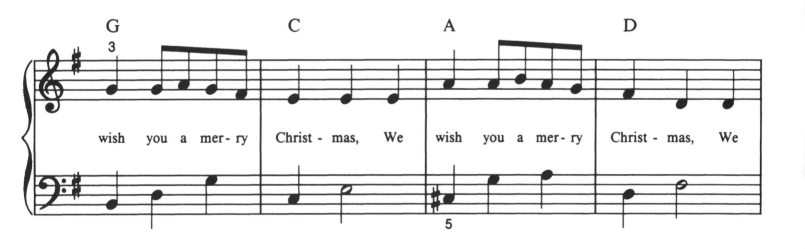

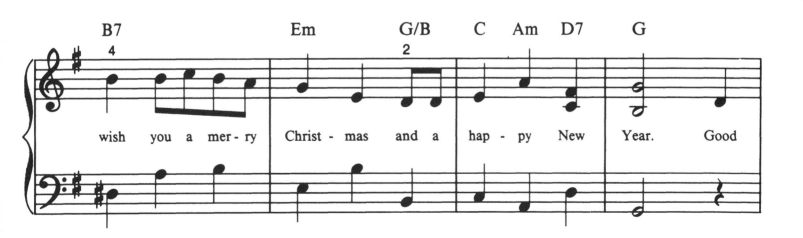

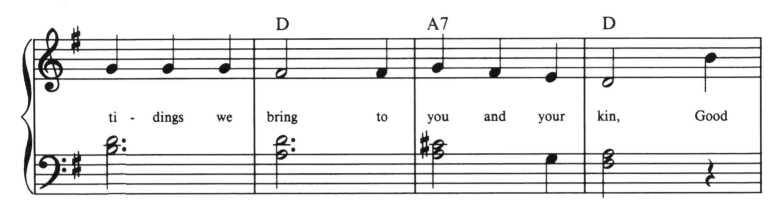

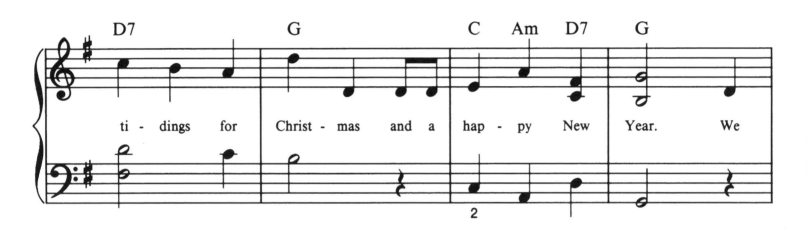

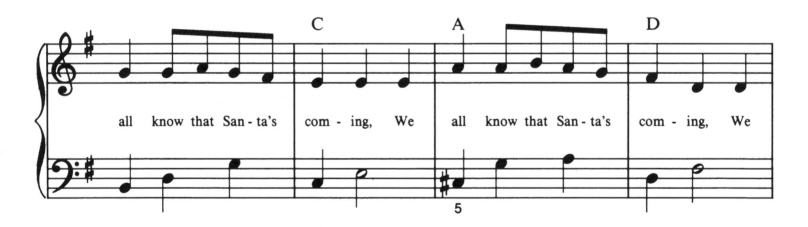

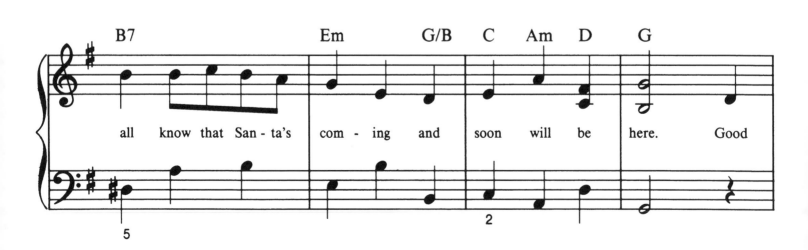

55

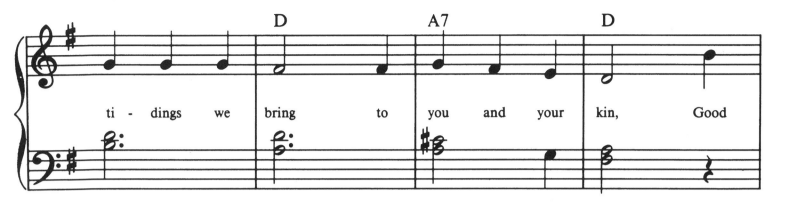

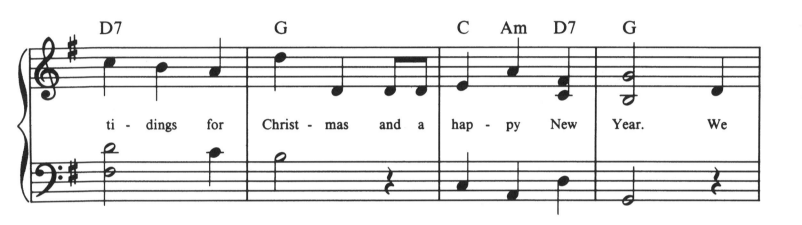

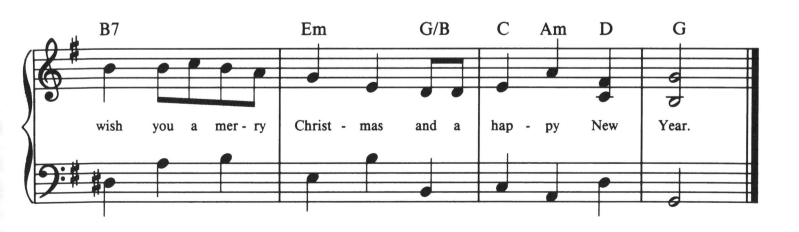